Summary of High Performance Habits
Brendon Burchard

Conversation Starters

By BookHabits

Please Note: This is an unofficial conversation starters guide. If you have not yet read the original work or would like to read it again, get the book here.

Copyright © 2017 by BookHabits. All Rights Reserved.

First Published in the United States of America 2017

We hope you enjoy this complementary guide from BookHabits.

Our mission is to aid readers and reading groups with quality, thought provoking material to in the discovery and discussions on some of today's favorite books.

Disclaimer / Terms of Use: Product names, logos, brands, and other trademarks featured or referred to within this publication are the property of their respective trademark holders and are not affiliated with BookHabits. The publisher and author make no representations or warranties with respect to the accuracy or completeness of these contents and disclaim all warranties such as warranties of fitness for a particular purpose. This guide is unofficial and unauthorized. It is not authorized, approved, licensed, or endorsed by the original book's author or publisher and any of their licensees or affiliates.

No part of this publication may be reproduced or retransmitted, electronic or mechanical, without the written permission of the publisher.

Tips for Using BookHabits Conversation Starters:

EVERY GOOD BOOK CONTAINS A WORLD FAR DEEPER THAN the surface of its pages. The characters and their world come alive through the words on the pages, yet the characters and its world still live on. Questions herein are designed to bring us beneath the surface of the page and invite us into the world that lives on. These questions can be used to:

- Foster a deeper understanding of the book
- Promote an atmosphere of discussion for groups
- Assist in the study of the book, either individually or corporately
- Explore unseen realms of the book as never seen before

About Us:

THROUGH YEARS OF EXPERIENCE AND FIELD EXPERTISE, from newspaper featured book clubs to local library chapters, *BookHabits* can bring your book discussion to life. Host your book party as we discuss some of today's most widely read books.

Table of Contents

Introducing *High Performace Habits* 6

Discussion Questions 13

Introducing the Author 34

Fireside Questions 39

Quiz Questions 50

Quiz Answers 63

Ways to Continue Your Reading 64

Introducing *High Performace Habits*

High Performance Habits: How Extraordinary People Become That Way by Brendon Burchard is a book about habits and how these help successful people achieve long-lasting success. It is a result of Burchard's research and coaching for the past 20 years. As a self-development coach, Burchard has worked with people who are top performers in their respective fields. He did research on them using surveys, interviews, assessment tools, and summed up the habits that made them outstanding performers.

Burchard promises readers that they will be equipped with the knowledge and tools that will make them succeed in their professional life. His suggestions are based on the experiences of high-achiever CEOs, TV and movie personalities, athletes, parents, and students. Burchard first defines high performance as going beyond what is widely accepted as standard and consistently sustaining this over a long period of time. He divides the six habits into personal and social habits.

The first habit, seek clarity, suggests having clear awareness of one's identity is key to self-esteem and eventually success. Knowing one's direction in life, what one wants to achieve, and ones strengths and weaknesses are key to achieving success. The second habit, generate energy, refers to mental, emotional and physical energy that need to be cultivated in order to be effective and powerful in work and life. Burchard cites studies showing that low energy affects happiness, enthusiasm, perception of one's success, confidence, influence on others, and diet and exercise habits. The third habit, raise necessity, refers to one of the most powerful motivating factor in humans -- performance necessity-- which moves people to act and achieve excellence. Burchard says high performers always feel a strong emotional commitment to what they do and what they want to achieve. Sticking to their high standards, no matter how discouraged they feel is key to their success. The fourth habit, which is the first under the social category, is increase productivity. Burchard cites studies that show high performers are higher in productivity and are happier, less stressed, and feel more rewarded, than people who devote so much time working but feel overburdened and unhappy. Unlike others, they do not compromise their well-being and their sense of balance. The fifth habit, develop influence, stresses how high performers teach their workmates how to think, challenge them to grow, and become role models themselves. The sixth habit, demonstrate courage, discusses how courage is a key factor among high performers' approach to work and life. They acknowledge and are thankful for the struggles they go through, they share their truths and ambitions no matter how vulnerable they feel, and they always have people important to them that they are willing to fight for. After discussing the six habits, Burchard cautions readers about the three traps that pull high performers down -- superiority, dissatisfaction, and neglect.

The book is divided into three sections -- Personal Habits, Social Habits, and Sustaining Success. The six important habits are defined and explained in the first two sections, and the last section concludes by stressing the importance of why a long-term success is part of the definition of high performance. Quotes from high performers like Ralph Waldo Emerson, Albert Einstein, and

Andy Warhol are given in every chapter to introduce the topic. The introduction opens with Aristotle's thoughts on excellence and habits. Burchard tells stories about his clients in order to provide actual examples of the concepts related to the six habits. He mentions their difficulties and struggles they face and why they ask for Burchard's help for their particular situations. His stories include dialogue and descriptions of the successful people he deals with. He also tells his own life story to stress the importance of knowing one's identity and self-defined purpose. After explaining the habit, he gives activities for readers to do in order for them to learn and fully embrace the habit. He provides charts and other tools that help keep track of the performance and improvement of the habits. For example, he suggests a one-page journal sheet to be filled out every Sunday evening for 12 weeks. He provides check lists to be accomplished. A summary guide is provided at the end of the book that condenses the book's main points. It opens with a quote from Abraham Lincoln about being good in ones chosen field. Endnotes are given at the end, citing sources, scientific studies, and clarifications. References cite supplemental research articles.

High Performance Habits is #1 bestseller in Amazon's list. It is also in the bestseller list of *Wall Street Journal*. Inc. Magazine believes the book is one of the best books people can read this year.

Discussion Questions

"Get Ready to Enter a New World"

Tip: Begin with questions dealing with broader issues to ensure ample time for quality discussions. Read through all discussion questions before engaging.

question 1

High Performance Habits is a result of Brendon Burchard's 20 years' work as a personal development coach. Would you trust his advice based on the experience he has? Why? Why not?

~~~

~~~

question 2

Burchard worked with top performers in the fields of business, entertainment, and sports. Who among his clients made a strong impression on you? Why? What are his performance difficulties that he/she needed help with?

~~~

~~~

question 3

Burchard defines high performance as going beyond what is widely accepted as standard and consistently sustaining this over a long period of time. Do you agree with his definition of high performance? Are there ideas you would like to add to this definition?

~~~

~~~

question 4

He adds that a high performer has many skills that he/she uses to sustain long-term achievements. Do you agree that developing ones skills is key to high performance? What skills do you want to develop? How does this relate to your academic/professional development?

~~~

question 5

The six habits essential for high performance include: seek clarity, generate energy, raise necessity, increase productivity, develop influence, and demonstrate courage. How did Burchard come up with these six? How did he do his research?

~~~

question 6

The book is divided into three sections -- Personal Habits, Social Habits, and Sustaining Success. The six important habits are defined and explained in the first two sections, and the last section concludes by stressing the importance of why a long-term success is part of the definition of high performance. Do you like the way the book is structured? Can you suggest ways to improve the structure?

~~~

question 7

Quotes from high performers like Ralph Waldo Emerson, Albert Einstein, and Andy Warhol are given in every chapter opening to introduce the topic. The introduction opens with Aristotle's thoughts on excellence and habits. Do you like the the use of quotations in the book? How do these relate to the theme or topic of the chapters they introduce?

~~~

~~~

question 8

Burchard tells stories about his clients in order to provide actual examples of the concepts related to the six habits. He mentions their difficulties and struggles they face and why they ask for Burchard's help for their particular situations. Do you like the way he wrote the clients' stories? What part of the storytelling do you like? What part do you think can be improved?

~~~

~~~

question 9

He also tells his own life story to stress the importance of knowing one's identity and self-defined purpose. Does his life story help to explain his ideas about identity? Do you have abetter understanding of identity and clarity as a result?

~~~

~~~

question 10

After explaining the habit, he gives activities for readers to do in order for them to learn and fully embrace the habit. What activities do you like most? Why?

~~~

question 11

He provides charts and other tools that help keep track of the performance and improvement of the habits. For example, he suggests a one-page journal sheet to be filled out. Are the charts useful for you? Do you think the tools are important?

~~~

question 12

The first habit, seek clarity, suggests having clear awareness of one's identity is key to self-esteem and eventually success. Knowing one's direction in life, what one wants to achieve, and ones strengths and weaknesses are keys to achieving success. Have you had a better understanding of your identity as a result of reading the book? Can you share your insights?

~~~

~~~

question 13

The second habit, generate energy, refers to mental, emotional and physical energy that need to be cultivated in order to be effective and powerful in work and life. What parts of your life need to be improved in order to generate more energy? How are you going to do this?

~~~

question 14

Burchard says high performers always feel a strong emotional commitment to what they do and what they want to achieve. Sticking to their high standards, no matter how discouraged they feel is key to their success. Do you have a strong emotional commitment to what you want to achieve? Why do you feel strongly about your project, job, or goal?

~~~

question 15

The sixth habit, demonstrate courage, discusses how courage is a key factor among high performers' approach to work and life. They acknowledge and are thankful for the struggles they go through. Have you faced difficulties in your work that made you want to give up? How did you deal with these? Could you have dealt with past difficulties in a better way?

~~~

question 16

Brendon Burchard is a #1 *New York Times* bestselling author. *High Performance Habits* is his latest book. Do you think this will be another bestseller? Why do you think his other books made him a bestselling author?

~~~

question 17

Inc. Magazine believes the book is one of the best books people can read this year. Would you recommend the book to your friends and family? Why? Why not?

~~~

~~~

question 18

An Amazon review disagrees with the book's goal to help high performers be happier in their work. The review says happiness will not give meaning or contentment to ones life. Do you agree with the review? Why? Why not?

~~~

question 19

A Goodreads review says the book could have been written in less than 100 pages. Do you think the book could be condensed into fewer pages? What parts can you shorten or delete?

question 20

Valuewalk.com review says some of Burchard's suggestions are "hokey" but many of them are true. Do you think some suggestions are hokey? If yes, can you cite them and explain why?

~~~

Introducing the Author

Brendon Burchard has authored six books, three of which made him a *New York Times* bestselling author. He has more than five million Facebook followers and is the world's highest paid trainer for motivation and marketing. His strong online presence, with over 100 million Youtube views, is proof of his marketing prowess. Over two million people have taken his online courses and video series. He says he learned his work ethic from his father, a US marine who had been to Vietnam three times. Burchard did odd jobs during his pre-college years--painting buildings, doing janitorial work, and as a clerk. When he was 19 years old, he almost died in a car accident. He had a moment of clarity during that brief moment when his body bore the impact of the crash. In that moment when he thought he was about to die, he asked himself three questions which eventually changed his life: "Did I live? Did I love? Did I matter?" Before the crash, he was a depressed and suicidal person, having been left by his college girlfriend. Fortunately, he survived the crash. After recuperating from his injuries, he went back to college, finished graduate studies and strove to become a better person. He started reading personal development books which taught him to be more conscientious and disciplined. While in school, many people heard his story of how he recovered from the car crash and how he became a better person as a result. He decided to write a book about it. The result was his first major book *Life's Golden Ticket: A Story About Second Chances.* The book was all about how people want to change and how they can achieve this if they are willing to pay the price. After reading the book, his father hugged him with tears in his eyes. However, he could not find a book agent who was interested in the book. He lost money trying to spread his message through workshops and events. An agent eventually got interested in the book but it was rejected by 15 publishers. It was then that he decided to study marketing to promote his own book. His next three books eventually became *New York Times* bestsellers. He is now a top marketing professional whose expertise is sought by leading CEOs and entrepreneurs. He says his marketing strategy for his books is different from how publishing houses do it; he sees his books as a means to increase service to others. His third book, *The Millionaire Messenger: Make a Difference and a Fortune Sharing Your Advice,* earned him $4 Million in book sales, events, and online courses. To sell his book, he did five videos and emailed his subscribers who shared the video to their own email lists. This alone did the marketing; no public relations through TV and mainstream media was done. He met another accident in 2011 when he was writing his fourth book. He lost control of an all-terrain vehicle which gave him massive injuries and a broken body. His brain and mental functions were affected and he couldn't proceed in his writing. This terrified him and it took him lots of willpower to get well and finish the book, through the help of his wife, doctor and friends.

Fireside Questions

"What would you do?"

Tip: These questions can be a fun exercise as it spurs creativity among the readers by allowing alternate scene endings and "if this was you" questions.

~~~

question 21

Brendon Burchard has authored six books, three of which made him a *New York Times* bestselling author. He is the world's highest paid trainer for motivation and marketing, and has a strong online presence. With this background, do you think he is the right person to write a book about high performance habits? Why do you think he chooses to write about a topic like high performance?

~~~

~~~

question 22

He has over 100 million Youtube views. Over two million people have taken his online courses and video series. What do you think of his online popularity? Why do you think millions view his videos?

~~~

question 23

When he was 19 years old, he almost died in a car accident. In that moment when he thought he was about to die, he asked himself three questions which eventually changed his life. Why do you think this is a life-changing experience for him? Does feeling close to your death change how you look at life?

~~~

question 24

He had a hard time getting an agent for his first book, and when one eventually got interested, the book was rejected by 15 publishers. It was then that he decided to study marketing to promote his own book. His next three books eventually became *New York Times* bestsellers. How do you feel about the difficulty he went through as he tried to get published? How did he overcome the difficulty?

~~~

~~~

question 25

He met another accident in 2011 when he was writing his fourth book. His brain and mental functions were affected and he couldn't proceed with his writing. This terrified him and it took him lots of willpower to get well. How do you feel about him getting over the debilitating effects of his accident? What attitude did he have to enable him to overcome?

~~~

~~~

question 26

Burchard survived his first accident when he was 19 years old. He tried to change his life for the better as a result of the accident. If you are the one who figured in an accident, how would you respond to having survived it? Will you change anything in your life?

~~~

~~~

question 27

He had a hard time getting an agent for his first book. Fifteen publishers turned it down. If you are Burchard how would you have reacted to the disappointments? What would you have done to overcome them?

~~~

~~~

question 28

Burchard tells stories about his clients to highlight habits that need changing or improving. If you are writing the book, whose story would you want your readers to know? What habit or attitude does the story highlight?

~~~

~ ~ ~

question 29

Quotes from high performers like Ralph Waldo Emerson, Albert Einstein, and Andy Warhol are given in every chapter to introduce the topic. If you are the writer, whose quotes would you include? Why are they significant to you?

~ ~ ~

~~~

question 30

Burchard interviewed top performers in the fields of business, entertainmet, and sports to gain insight on their habits. If you are the writer, who are the top performers that you would like to interview? Why?

~~~

Quiz Questions

"Ready to Announce the Winners?"

Tip: Create a leaderboard and track scores to see who gets the most correct answers. Winners required. Prizes optional.

~~~

quiz question 1

High Performance Habits is a result of Buchard's research and coaching for the past years.

~~~

quiz question 2

The third habit, _____, refers to one of the most powerful motivating factor in humans -- performance necessity-- which moves people to act and achieve excellence. Buchard says high performers always feel a strong emotional commitment to what they do and what they want to achieve.

~~~

quiz question 3

The fifth habit,_____ , stresses how high performers teach their workmates how to think, challenge them to grow, and become role models themselves.

~~~

~~~

quiz question 4

True or False: The first habit, seek clarity, suggests having clear awareness of one's identity. It is is the key to self-esteem and eventually success. it involves knowing one's direction in life, what one wants to achieve, and ones strengths and weaknesses.

~~~

quiz question 5

True or False: Burchard cites studies that show high performers are higher in productivity and are happier, less stressed, and feel more rewarded, than people who devote so much time working but feel overburdened and unhappy.

~~~

quiz question 6

True or False: Burchard says mental, emotional and physical energy need not be cultivated. One can be effective and powerful in work and life without them.

~~~

~~~

quiz question 7

True or False: Burchard cautions readers about the three traps that pull high performers down -- superiority, dissatisfaction, and laziness.

~~~

~~~

quiz question 8

Brendon Burchard has authored _____ books, three of which made him a *New York Times* bestselling author.

~~~

~~~

quiz question 9

His first book was rejected by ____ publishers. It was then that he decided to study marketing to promote his own book.

~~~

~~~

quiz question 10

True or False: He almost died in a car accident. In that moment when he thought he was about to die, he asked himself three questions which eventually changed his life: "Did I live? Did I love? Did I matter?"

~~~

quiz question 11

True or False: He decided to write a book about his experience in surviving the car crash. His first major book is called *Surviving the Crash*.

~~~

quiz question 12

True or False: After his first book, his next three books became *New York Times* bestsellers.

~~~

Quiz Answers

1. 20
2. raise necessity
3. develop influence
4. True
5. True
6. False
7. False
8. six
9. 15
10. True
11. False
12. True

Ways to Continue Your Reading

EVERY month, our team runs through a wide selection of books to pick the best titles for readers and reading groups, and promotes these titles to our thousands of readers – sometimes with free downloads, sale dates, and additional brochures.

If you have not yet read the original work or would like to read it again, get the book here.

Want to register yourself or a book group? It's free and takes 1-click.

Register here.

On the Next Page...

Please write us your reviews! Any length would be fine but we'd appreciate hearing you more! We'd be SO grateful.

Till next time,

BookHabits

"Loving Books is Actually a Habit"

CPSIA information can be obtained
at www.ICGtesting.com
Printed in the USA
LVHW092314101019
633881LV00001BA/188/P